Making Meaning®

THIRD EDITION

Making Meaning is a registered trademark of Center for the Collaborative Classroom.

Center for the Collaborative Classroom wishes to thank the following authors, agents, and publishers for their permission to reprint materials included in this program. Every effort has been made to trace the ownership of copyrighted material and to make full acknowledgment of its use. If errors or omissions have occurred, they will be corrected in subsequent printings, provided that notification is submitted in writing to the publisher.

Excerpt from *Cherries and Cherry Pits* by Vera Williams. Text copyright © 1986 by Vera Williams. Used by permission of HarperCollins Publishers. Excerpts from *Julius, the Baby of the World* by Kevin Henkes. Copyright © 1990 by Kevin Henkes. Used by permission of HarperCollins Publishers. Excerpt from *A Day's Work* by Eve Bunting. Text copyright © 1994 by Eve Bunting. Reprinted by permission of Clarion Books, an imprint of Houghton Mifflin Harcourt Publishing Company. All rights reserved. Excerpt from *Mailing May* by Michael O. Tunnell. Text copyright © 1997 by Michael O. Tunnell. Used with the permission of Greenwillow Books. Excerpts from *Brave Irene*. Copyright © 1986 by William Steig. Reprinted by permission of Farrar, Straus and Giroux, LLC. All rights reserved. Excerpt from *Brave Harriet* by Marissa Moss. Text copyright © 2001 by Marissa Moss. Reprinted by permission of Houghton Mifflin Harcourt Publishing Company. All rights reserved. Excerpt from *Wilma Unlimited: How Wilma Rudolph Became the World's Fastest Woman* by Kathleen Krull. Copyright © 1996 by Kathleen Krull. Reprinted by permission of Houghton Mifflin Company. All rights reserved. Text excerpt from *Sonia Sotomayor: A Judge Grows in the Bronx* by Jonah Winter. Text copyright © 2003 by Jonah Winter. Reprinted with the permission of Atheneum Books for Young Readers, an imprint of Simon & Schuster Children's Publishing Division. Excerpts from the work titled *Morning Meals Around the World* by Maryellen Gregoire. Copyright © 2004 by Capstone Press. All rights reserved. Excerpt from the work titled *Homes* by Chris Oxlade. Copyright © 2012 by Capstone Press. All rights reserved. Photo of kids jumping hopscotch on p. 34 copyright © 1999–2015 Getty Images, Inc./Image Source. All rights reserved. Photo of girl drawing hopscotch board on p. 34 copyright © 1999–2015 Getty Images, Inc./Taxi. All rights reserved. Image of paper cranes on top of p.36 copyright © iStockphoto.com/Boboling. Photo of origami ball on p. 37 copyright © 2003–2014 Shutterstock, Inc./David Hsu. Image of paper cranes on p. 37 copyright © 2003–2015 Shutterstock, Inc./Radu Razvan. Photo of children playing double Dutch on p. 38 copyright © Richard Levine/Alamy. Background art on pp. 38–39 © 2003–2015 Shutterstock, Inc./freesoulproduction. Excerpts from *Flashy, Fantastic Rainforest Frogs* by Dorothy Hinshaw Patent. Copyright © 1997 by Dorothy Hinshaw Patent. Reprinted by arrangement with Walker & Co. "Polar Bears in Peril" by Elizabeth Winchester, November 2, 2012, from the pages of **TIME for Kids**. Copyright © 2012 by Time Inc. All rights reserved. Reprinted/translated from **TIME for Kids** and published with permission of Time Inc. Reproduction in any manner in any language in whole or in part without written permission is prohibited. Photo of polar bear swimming on p. xx copyright © 2015 Thinkstock fotokon. All rights reserved. Photo of polar bear on ice on p. xx copyright © 2003©2015 Shutterstock, Inc./Shchipkova Elena. Illustration of children on p. xx copyright © 1999–2015 Getty Images, Inc./McMillan Digital Art. All rights reserved. Photo of girls running on p. xx copyright © Fotosearch, LLC. All rights reserved. Background art on p. xx copyright © 2003–2015 Shutterstock, Inc./JMCM. Picture of boy on p. xx copyright © 2003–2015 Shutterstock, Inc./Monkey Business Images. Picture of child and parent on p. xx copyright © 2003–2015 Shutterstock, Inc./Monkey Business Images. Background art on p. xx copyright © 2003–2015 Shutterstock, Inc./Srdjan 111. Photo of girl on p. xx copyright © 2003–2015 Shutterstock, Inc./Ollyy. Photo of parent and child on p. xx copyright © 2015 Thinkstock. All rights reserved. Excerpts from *Lifetimes* by David L. Rice, illustrated by Michael Maydak. Text copyright © 1997 by David L. Rice. Used by permission of Dawn Publications. Excerpts from "The Young Rooster," "The Mouse at the Seashore," and "The Camel Dances" from *Fables* by Arnold Lobel. Copyright © 1980 by Arnold Lobel. Used by permission of HarperCollins Publishers. Excerpt from *Possum's Tail* from *Pushing Up the Sky* by Joseph Bruchac, copyright © 2000 by Joseph Bruchac. Used by permission of Dial Books for Young Readers, a division of Penguin Group (USA) LLC.

All articles and texts reproduced in this manual and not referenced with a credit line above were created by Center for the Collaborative Classroom.

Cover illustration by Michael Wertz, copyright © Center for the Collaborative Classroom

Center for the Collaborative Classroom
1001 Marina Village Parkway, Suite 110
Alameda, CA 94501
(800) 666-7270; fax: (510) 464-3670
collaborativeclassroom.org

ISBN 978-1-61003-709-9

Printed in the United States of America

10 11 12 13 BNG 24 23 22 21 20 19

Making Meaning®

THIRD EDITION

Draw your mental image of the woman on the train.

Excerpt from *Cherries and Cherry Pits* by Vera B. Williams

Name:

Underline words or phrases that helped you create your mental image.

THIS is the train seat. And THIS is a tiny white woman sitting on the train seat. She is almost as short as I am, but she is a grandmother. On her head is a black hat with a pink flower, like a rose flower. It has shiny green leaves, like the leaves in my uncle's florist shop. On her feet are old, old shoes. These are the buckles. And in her lap is a big black pocketbook. And in the pocketbook is a bag.

How I Visualized

Aunt Flossie's Hats (and Crab Cakes Later)

**Draw a part of the story you visualized clearly.
Describe what you drew on the lines below.**

_____

_____

_____

_____

Excerpt from *Julius, the Baby of the World* (1) by Kevin Henkes

Name:

Underline clues about how Lilly feels.

Before Julius was born, Lilly was the best big sister in the world.
She gave him things.
She told him secrets.
And she sang lullabies to him every night.

After Julius was born, it was a different story.
Lilly took her things back.
She pinched his tail.
And she yelled insulting comments into his crib.
"I am the queen," said Lilly. "And I hate Julius."

Underline clues about how Lilly feels.

"You're talking about my brother," said Lilly. "And for your information, his nose is shiny, his eyes are sparkly, and his fur smells like perfume."

Cousin Garland was speechless.

"He can blow bubbles," continued Lilly. "He can babble and gurgle. And he can scream better than anyone."

Cousin Garland tried to slink out of the room.

"Stop!" said Lilly. "I am the queen. Watch me closely."

Lilly picked up Julius.

She kissed his wet pink nose.

She admired his small black eyes.

And she stroked his sweet white fur.

Character Web
for Grace

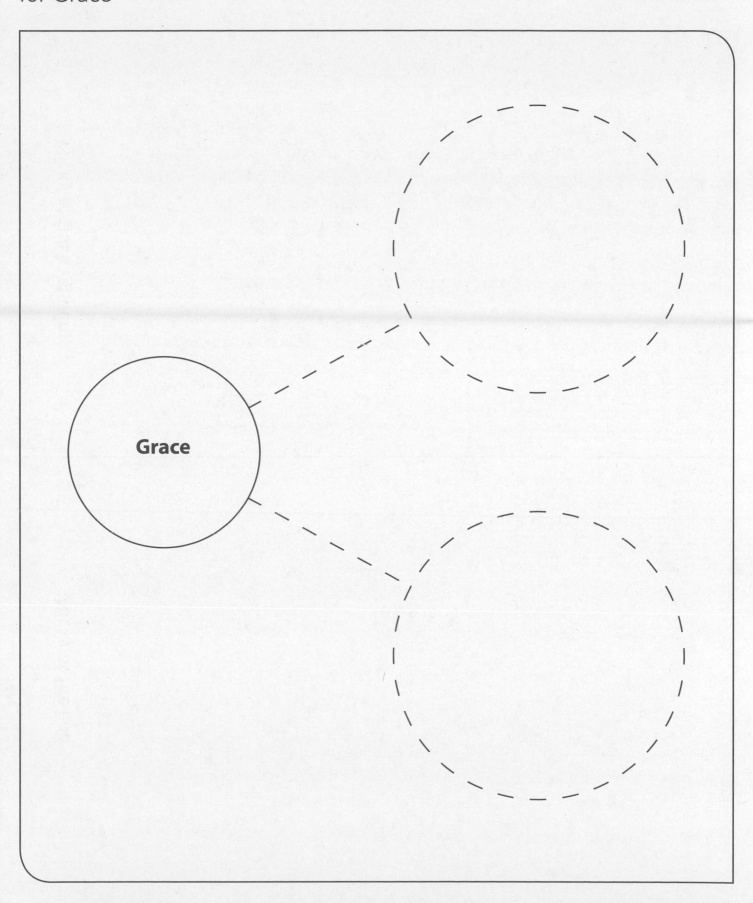

Grace

Double-entry Journal

About Nicky

Name:

Nicky at the beginning

Nicky at the end

Double-entry Journal

About Alexander

Alexander at the end

Alexander at the beginning

© Center for the Collaborative Classroom

Stop and Ask Questions
About *A Day's Work*

Name:

At each stop, write your questions in the box.

 1

 2

 3

STOP **4**

from *A Day's Work*

by Eve Bunting

"Look," he said. "If you need money I'll give you half now." He began to pull his wallet from his pocket but Abuelo held up his hand.

"Tell him we take the pay tomorrow, when we finish."

Francisco's grandfather and Ben looked at each other and words seemed to pass between them, though there were no words. Ben slid his wallet back into his pocket.

Francisco sighed. The lie had taken the chorizos, too.

"Tomorrow then. Six A.M.," Ben said. "And tell your grandfather I can always use a good man—for more than just one day's work."

Francisco gave a hop of excitement. More than just a day's work!

Ben was still speaking. "The important things your grandfather knows already. And I can teach him gardening."

Francisco nodded. He understood. He would tell his grandfather, and he would tell him something else. He, Francisco, had begun to learn the important things, too.

Francisco took his grandfather's cold, rough hand in his. "Let's go home, Abuelo," he said.

Stop and Ask Questions

Name:

About _____

At each stop, write your questions in the box.

Before Reading

 STOP **1**

STOP **2**

STOP **3**

Stop and Ask Questions

About *Mailing May*

Name:

At each stop, write your questions in the box.

 1

 2

 3

 4

Excerpt

from *Mailing May*
by Michael O. Tunnell

Whenever Leonard had a free minute, he'd take me to the door for a look. My, oh, my, what sights there were to see! Why, we hung on the edge of mountainsides and crawled through tunnels. We crossed deep valleys on top of tall, spidery trestles that Leonard called "steel on stilts."

Then long about Lapwai Canyon, where the train track twists back and forth down the mountain, I began to feel somewhat less adventuresome. Instead, I was feeling dizzy and weak in the stomach. I was about to run to get some fresh air when I heard an angry voice at the door.

How I Visualized

Mailing May

**Draw a picture of what May sees from the mail car of the train.
Describe your drawing on the lines below.**

_____

_____

_____

_____

Stop and Ask Questions

About _____

At each stop, write your questions in the box.

 1

 2

 3

Stop and Ask Questions

About *Brave Irene*

At each stop, write your questions in the box.

STOP 1

STOP 2

STOP 3

STOP 4

from *Brave Irene*
by William Steig

Cold snow sifted into her boots and chilled her feet. She pushed out her lip and hurried on. This was an important errand.

She laid the box down and climbed aboard. But it pressed into the snow and stuck. She tried again, and this time, instead of climbing on, she leaped. The box shot forward, like a sled.

Stop and Ask Questions

About _____

Name: _____

At each stop, write your questions in the box.

 STOP 1

 STOP 2

STOP 3

from *Brave Harriet*
by Marissa Moss

This story is based on the life of Harriet Quimby, the first American woman to receive a pilot's license and the first woman to fly solo across the English Channel. The descriptions of her flight are taken from the newspaper article she wrote about it as a reporter for the *New York Herald*. When Harriet made her flight in 1912, the "aeroplane" was still young as a machine, a wooden open-air contraption that looked about as strong as a good box kite. More than a decade would pass before planes would have the enclosed metal cockpits that we associate with Amelia Earhart and Charles Lindbergh. But there already existed a breed of daredevil pilots, and Harriet was among them. She made a name as an exhibition flier, performing for the inauguration of the president of Mexico in 1911, then setting her sights on crossing the English Channel.

Gustav Hamel, an early aviator who had already successfully crossed the Channel, did actually offer to trade places with Harriet, so convinced was he that the flight was beyond a woman's ability. Harriet proved him wrong, and she worked hard to promote commercial aviation and a place for women within it. She even foresaw a day when passengers would regularly be carried on flights of fifty or sixty miles!

Unfortunately for Harriet, her landing in France coincided with the news of the sinking of the *Titanic*. The newspapers were filled with news of the tragedy, and Harriet's feat didn't even make the back pages of the *New York Herald*. She was determined to keep flying, however, and died doing what she loved, soaring into the blue. The *Boston Post* wrote of her death: "Ambitious to be among the pathfinders, she took her chances like a man and died like one." Her gravestone expresses that daring as well: THERE IS NO REASON TO BE AFRAID.

Double-entry Journal

About *Brave Harriet*

Name:

What I Wonder

What I Learned

Double-entry Journal

About _____

What I Learned

What I Wonder

from *Wilma Unlimited*

by Kathleen Krull

Wilma Rudolph became, at age twenty, the first American woman to win three gold medals at a single Olympics. When she returned home from Rome, her family was waiting for her, and so was all of Clarksville, Tennessee. The huge parade and banquet held in her honor were the first events in the town's history to include both blacks and whites. . . .

After she retired from her career as a runner in 1962, Wilma became a second-grade teacher and a high school coach. She remained a much-admired celebrity, but to prove that there was more to her than just running, she started a company called Wilma Unlimited that gave her opportunities to travel, lecture, and support causes she believed in. Later she founded the nonprofit Wilma Rudolph Foundation to nurture young athletes and to teach them that they, too, can succeed despite all odds against them. The story of all she overcame in order to win at the Olympics has inspired thousands of young athletes, especially women.

Wilma Rudolph died in 1994.

Double-entry Journal

About *Wilma Unlimited*

Name:

What I Learned

What I Wonder

from *Sonia Sotomayor*
by Jonah Winter

In America, we like to believe that anyone—regardless of their background—can achieve great things. It's called the American Dream, and Sonia Sotomayor is a wonderful example of it, rising from humble beginnings to become the first Latin-American Supreme Court justice. Hers is a very inspiring—and very American—story, but not all of it could fit in this book. Here are a few extra details and explanations of her life, her struggle, and her success.

Sonia Maria Sotomayor was born on June 25, 1954 in a rough part of New York City called the South Bronx. When she was three years old, her family moved from a tenement building to the Bronxdale Houses. Like most project tenants, Sonia's family did not have a lot of money, but still she knew they were more fortunate than her cousins and aunts and uncles back in Puerto Rico, whom she visited every summer. Home in America, Sonia attended good schools, which her mother worked very hard to send her to, and enjoyed small indulgences, like going to see baseball games at Yankee Stadium.

Before being appointed to the Supreme Court, Justice Sotomayor was a lawyer and a judge and held many different positions. Her first job after law school was as the assistant district attorney in Manhattan (a district attorney is a lawyer who prosecutes criminals). She held this position from 1979 to 1984 and then decided to work as a lawyer for a law firm. There, she sometimes went with the police on dangerous raids. It's even been said that she once rode on the back of a motorcycle while chasing a criminal through Chinatown! Finally, in 1992, she fulfilled her lifelong dream of becoming a judge! She was appointed to the U.S. District Court for the Southern District of

(continues)

New York by President George H. W. Bush, and she was the youngest judge (and the first Latin American) ever to be appointed to this court. As a district court judge, she was well known (and liked!) for ending a Major League Baseball strike that threatened to ruin the 1995 season for fans all over America. Some say she saved baseball!

In 1997, Justice Sotomayor was nominated to the U.S. Court of Appeals for the Second Circuit, and in 1998 she was confirmed by the Senate as a judge to this very important court. But of course, how she truly made history was by becoming a Supreme Court justice. Not only is she the first Latin American to have a seat in America's highest court, she also came to the position with more legal experience as a federal judge than any current Supreme Court justice at the time of their nominations. Pretty impressive!

Although Justice Sotomayor has become a very important and successful adult, some things haven't changed since her childhood in the South Bronx. She still takes shots for her diabetes every day, and she still goes to see her beloved New York Yankees. She still likes to listen to merengue music (which actually has Dominican rather than Puerto Rican roots), and she still loves her family more than anything in the world. Justice Sotomayor is a wonderful aunt, and she buys her nephews and nieces so many presents that she has little money left over for herself. Like mother, like daughter!

Text excerpt from *Sonia Sotomayor: A Judge Grows in the Bronx* by Jonah Winter. Text copyright © 2003 by Jonah Winter. Reprinted with the permission of Atheneum Books for Young Readers, an imprint of Simon & Schuster Children's Publishing Division.

Double-entry Journal

About *Sonia Sotomayor*

Name:

What I Wonder

What I Learned

Table of Contents from *Morning Meals Around the World*

by Maryellen Gregoire

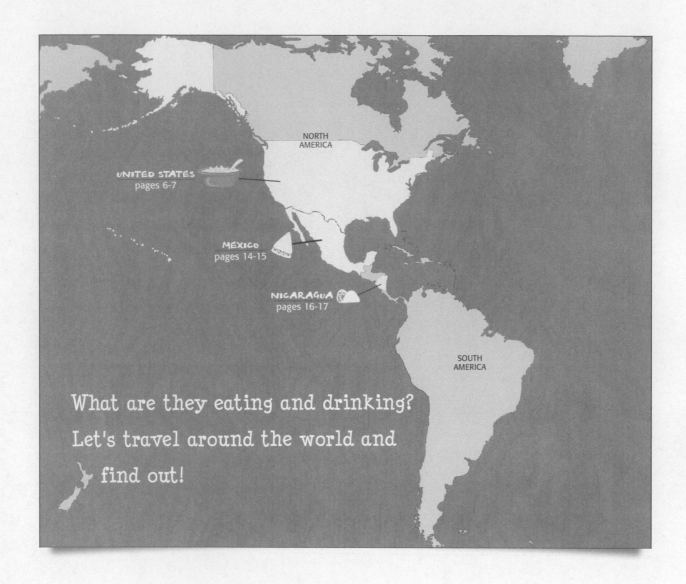

What are they eating and drinking?
Let's travel around the world and
find out!

Table of Contents from *Morning Meals Around the World*

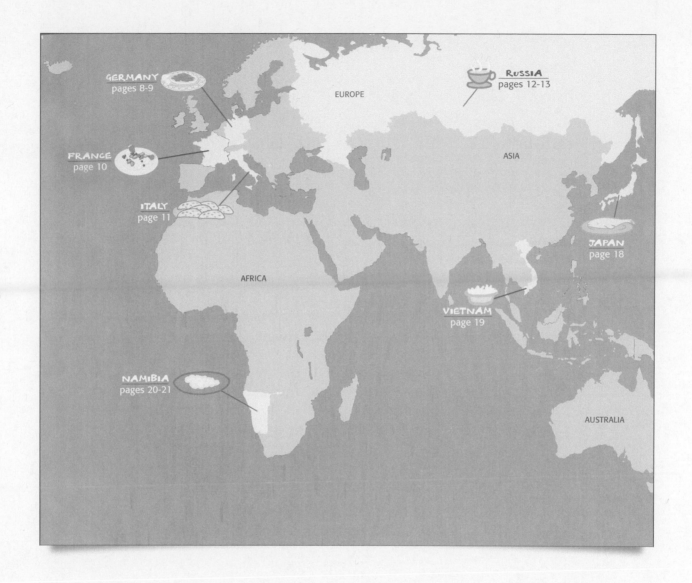

Index from *Morning Meals Around the World*

by Maryellen Gregoire

Index

biscotti, 11

caffe latte, 11

crepes, 10

France, 5, 10

gallo pinto, 16–17

Germany, 5, 8–9

Italy, 5, 11

Japan, 5, 18

Mexico, 4, 14–15

Namibia, 5, 20–21

Nicaragua, 4, 16–17

Pfannkuchen, 8

Russia, 5, 12–13

Taiwan, 24

United States, 4, 6–7

Vietnam, 5, 19

Diagram from *Homes*

by Chris Oxlade

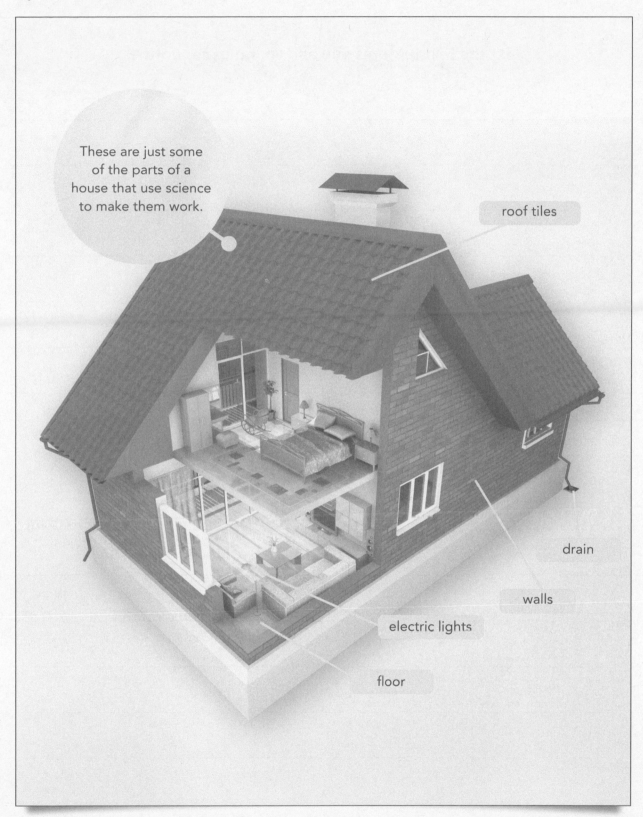

These are just some of the parts of a house that use science to make them work.

roof tiles

drain

walls

electric lights

floor

Text Features

List the text features you and your partner notice.

_____

_____

_____

_____

_____

_____

_____

_____

_____

_____

_____

_____

Text Features

Three Things I Learned

from ▶ Text Features in the Articles

What information can you find in the text features in the articles on pages 34–39? Write three things you learned.

_____

_____

_____

_____

_____

_____

_____

_____

_____

_____

_____

_____

HOP TO IT:
Fancy Footwork

Looking for a fun outdoor game? Grab a piece of chalk, a stone, and a friend. What can you play? Hopscotch!

The first hopscotch courts were made around 2,000 years ago. Imagine a hopscotch court 100 feet long—about the length of a professional basketball court. That's how big the first courts were. They were not made for fun, either. Instead, they were used for a training exercise. Roman soldiers would dress in heavy armor and run from one end of the court to the other and back again. This exercise helped them stay quick on their feet.

Hopping Around the World

Roman children watched the soldiers and imitated them. They drew smaller courts on the ground with chalk and made their own rules. Hopscotch became a game! Their game was simple to learn yet challenging to play. It quickly became popular throughout Europe. Later, it spread to Asia and America.

In every country, children changed the game in their own way. In France, the court is drawn in the shape of a snail. In Bolivia, the squares in the court are named for the days of the week. In the United States, hopscotch is played in many ways. For example, in Alaska, the squares are not named or numbered.

Hopscotch is a simple game with a long history. Over the centuries, it has spread all over the world. Hopscotch proves that the simplest games are often the most popular.

34

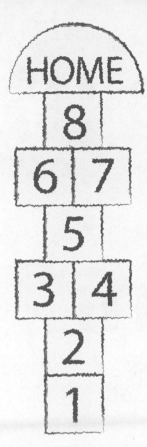

A traditional hopscotch court has eight or ten squares. Once you have learned how to play and how to hop on one leg, it's a lot of fun.

How to Play

To play a game of traditional hopscotch, all you need is one traditional hopscotch court (you can draw one with chalk), one stone, and two or more people. Make sure all the players know these rules:

- A player must toss the stone into every square in sequence.
- Players must land with only one foot in any square.
- Players can't land on a line.
- Players can't hop into any square that is holding the stone.
- A player's turn ends if he or she breaks any of the above rules or if the stone doesn't land in the right square when it is tossed.

When it's your turn, toss the stone into square 1 and then hop on one leg into square 2. Next, jump into squares 3 and 4 so that your left foot is in square 3 and your right foot is in square 4. Continue to hop and jump to the end of the court (making sure only one foot lands in each square!). Now, turn around in the "home" square and hop back to the beginning of the court, pausing to pick up the stone in square 1 before you hop out.

Once you've completed the first pass through the court, toss the stone into square 2 and hop through the court again, hopping over the square that has your stone in it and picking up the stone on your way back. Continue throwing your stone into the next square and hopping through the court again until you step on a line or fall. Then it's the next player's turn! When it's your turn again, continue by tossing the stone into the last square you aimed for. The first player who is able to hop through the course with his or her stone in the last square is the winner!

Hopping in France

In the French hopscotch game, no stone is used. The player hops through the spiral shape, from square 1 to square 17. Then the player hops back to the beginning, chooses a square, and writes his or her initials inside it. The other players must hop over this square. The game is over when it becomes too hard for anyone to hop to the center. The player whose initials are written inside the most squares is the winner.

An Alaskan Pastime

In the Alaskan version of hopscotch, the court has a "side pocket." The player stands inside the side pocket and tosses the stone into the first square. The player then hops diagonally into the second square (skipping the square holding the stone) and hops to the end of the court. The player hops back to the second square, picks up the stone, hops out, and gives the stone to the next player. That player tosses the stone into the second square and repeats the pattern. If a player tosses the stone and it does not land in a square, that player is out. The players repeat the pattern until one person is left—the winner!

In France, hopscotch courts are shaped like snail shells.

An Alaskan hopscotch court has a side pocket.

Origami
The Art of Japanese Paper Folding

Could you fold a square of paper into a graceful fish or a long-stemmed flower? Origami, or Japanese paper folding, is an art form practiced by many people. In origami, a simple sheet of paper can become a spectacular piece of art.

Japan is an island country that lies near the east coasts of Russia, Korea, and China. It is made up of four major islands.

Ancient Art Form, Modern Appeal

Paper was invented in China and brought to Japan around the year 500. Because paper was rare back then, paper decorations were reserved for special ceremonies. As paper became more common, people started to make paper models for fun. By the 1800s, children in Japan and Europe were learning the art of folding paper into interesting shapes.

Traditionally, origami objects are created using square pieces of paper that range in size from 1 to 15 inches wide. Six inches is one of the most common sizes. The paper is usually colored or patterned on one or both sides. The paper square is not usually cut or glued but is shaped by making a series of creases and folds. Some artists use wet paper to achieve a more rounded look; others experiment with unusual materials, such as cloth, wire, sheet metal, and even toilet paper.

36

A Worldwide Craze

Today, there are fans of origami worldwide. The most popular shapes are still traditional Japanese models, such as flowers and birds, but many people are inspired by more unusual-looking life-forms, such as scorpions, armadillos, and horned beetles.

Some people submit their paper creations to origami contests. Some origami contests have a theme such as plants or prehistoric animals. In other contests, there are categories such as best original design, best technical folding, and best miniature model. Winners of the Massachusetts Institute of Technology origami contest have included precise models of a butterfly, a sailboat, and a gold-colored beaver.

Origami is a tradition that has been passed on through many generations. Artists fold origami to express themselves. Scientists and engineers use it to explore shapes and angles to invent new technology. Teachers sometimes use origami as a tool to help kids learn math. And many people fold paper just because it's fun.

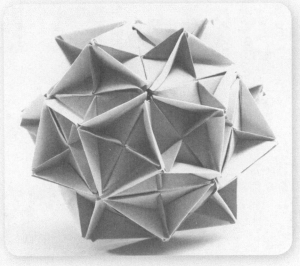

Folding origami can be a fun challenge. Some complicated origami figures are constructed using several sheets of paper.

One Thousand Paper Cranes

In the city of Hiroshima, Japan, people bring thousands of paper cranes to a memorial park every year. They do this to remember a girl named Sadako Sasaki. After World War II (1939–1945), Sadako became ill with leukemia, a form of cancer. She had heard the legend that if a person folds 1,000 paper cranes, he or she will be granted one wish. Her wish was to become healthy again.

Sadako decided to fold 1,000 paper cranes. For months, she kept folding and folding, but on October 25, 1955, she died, with 350 cranes left to make. Her friends completed the remaining cranes for her. Sadako's determination to finish her project has come to stand for a wish for peace. Today, people across the world fold paper cranes and string them into chains. They send them to the memorial park to remember Sadako's dream.

A 1,000-crane chain takes a long time for one person to make, but it can be completed quickly if many people join in.

Jump Rope
Then and Now

Double Dutch is one of the most popular ways to jump rope.

Have you ever jumped rope? It's a fun activity that kids do in schoolyards and on sidewalks everywhere! Did you know that people have been jumping rope for a long, long time? In fact, the origins of jumping rope go back thousands of years, but it has come a long way since then.

No one knows for sure when and how jumping rope started. Some say the game originated in Egypt more than 3,000 years ago, when the Egyptians jumped over vines as a form of play. What we do know is that jumping rope began in ancient times and has traveled around the world.

Coming to America

It is believed that Dutch settlers brought jumping rope to the American colonies in the 1600s. Some say it was the Dutch who developed a new way to jump called "double Dutch," which is one of the more popular—and difficult—jumping games today. In this game, two people hold two ropes, one end of each rope in each hand, and turn them in opposite directions as jumpers jump over both ropes.

Three hundred years later, in the 1940s and 1950s, jumping rope became popular with kids in America's cities. At that time, young jumpers used jump rope as a form of play because it required only a rope and almost anyone could learn how to do it.

Later, in the 1970s, Americans became more and more concerned with being fit and healthy. This led to an increased interest in jumping rope as a form of physical fitness. During this time, two New York City police officers, David A. Walker and Ulysses Williams, turned double Dutch into a world-class sport. On February 14, 1974, nearly 600 fifth-, sixth-, seventh-, and eighth-grade students participated in the first double Dutch tournament ever held.

Jumping Today

Today, jumping rope is seen as a fun way for both kids and grown-ups to play and exercise, which has resulted in the formation of many jump rope organizations and clubs. There are also special jump rope events, including some that raise money for charities. In 1978, Jean Barkow, a high school physical education teacher, held a "Jump-Rope-A-Thon," which raised $2,032 for the American Heart Association. Since then, Barkow's annual event, now called Jump Rope for Heart, has raised more than $750 million!

People jump rope competitively, as well. Competitive jumpers work on their speed and fancy jumping moves. In 2012, Jolien Kempeneer set a world record by jumping 204 times in 30 seconds.

Interested in having some fun with your friends, getting some exercise, or enjoying some serious competition? Grab a rope and get jumping!

Jump Rope Songs

Jump rope can include singing songs in rhythm with the jumping and rope turning. Often, the words of these songs include instructions to the jumpers on how to jump and when to jump into and out of the turning rope.

Teddy Bear, teddy bear,
Turn around. *[Jumper turns in a circle.]*
Teddy Bear, teddy bear,
Touch the ground. *[Jumper touches the ground.]*
Teddy Bear, teddy bear,
Tie your shoe. *[Jumper touches his or her shoe.]*
Teddy Bear, teddy bear,
How old are you?
1, 2, 3, 4, 5 . . . *[Continue counting out loud. The jumper jumps out when their age is called.]*

Important Dates in Modern Jump Rope History

February 1974: The first double Dutch tournament is held.

September 1979: The American Heart Association turns Barkow's idea into a national school event, Jump Rope for Heart.

July 2006: The FISAC-IRSF World Rope Skipping Championships event is held in Toronto, Canada.

March 2014: Jump Rope for Heart celebrates raising more than $750 million since it was started 35 years ago.

March 1978: Jean Barkow holds a Jump-Rope-A-Thon at Riverside High School in Milwaukee, Wisconsin.

October 1995: The organization USA Jump Rope is formed to promote jumping rope as a form of exercise and a competitive sport.

February 2007: The fourth Asian Rope Skipping Championships event is held in New Delhi, India.

June 2014: The U.S. National Jump Rope Championship is held in Long Beach, California.

1970 1980 1990 2000 2010

Examples of Functional Texts

Open Hours

Monday–Friday:	9 A.M.–7 P.M.
Saturday:	9 A.M.–6 P.M.
Sunday:	10 A.M.–5 P.M.

CAROUSEL

1 ride = 3 tickets

2 rides = 5 tickets

3 rides = 7 tickets

YIELD

☞ *PLEASE*

PICK UP AFTER YOUR DOG

Thank You!

Dear Michael,
Thank you for coming to my party!
From, Cheri

California-Grown Oranges
Organic

BUBBLES

For Ages 3 and Up

Warning: Keep away from eyes. Soap may cause stinging.

```
         CORNER MARKET
APPLES              $4.08
BREAD               $3.99
WATER               $1.99
BROCCOLI            $4.27
RICE                $2.19

Subtotal           $16.52
Tax                 $1.32
Total              $17.84

   January 11 5:42 pm
```

YOU'RE INVITED!

BRADY IS 8!

PICNIC BIRTHDAY PARTY

DATE: Saturday, June 8th
TIME: 11:00 A.M.
PLACE: Central Park
RSVP by May 31st

This Week's Helpers

Feed Fish	*David*
Pass Out Paper	*Emma*
Water Plants	*Molly*
Wipe Tables	*Chris*

7-day Weather Forecast

MON	TUES	WED	THURS	FRI	SAT	SUN
High: **71** Low: **59**	High: **69** Low: **57**	High: **71** Low: **61**	High: **70** Low: **59**	High: **68** Low: **56**	High: **68** Low: **58**	High: **69** Low: **57**
SUNNY	SUNNY	PARTIAL CLOUDS	PARTIAL CLOUDS	RAIN	PARTIAL CLOUDS	SUNNY

How to Make
A PAPER AIRPLANE

1. Fold the sheet of paper in half vertically. Open the paper.

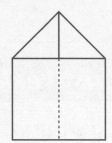

2. Fold the top left and right corners down so that they align with the center fold and form triangles.

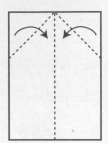

3. Fold the left and right corners in so that they align at the center fold and again form triangles.

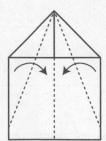

4. Fold the paper in half, keeping the folds from steps 1, 2, and 3 on the inside.

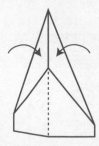

5. Fold the top wing in half so that the edge of the wing aligns with the rudder.

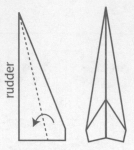

6. Flip the plane over and fold the other wing in half so that the edge of the wing aligns with the rudder.

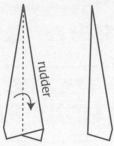

7. Open the plane and fold up the tips at the back of the wings to help the plane fly better.

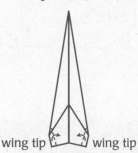

wing tip   wing tip   rudder

wings

wing tips

rudder

Flying Tips:

- If your plane dives and crashes, fold the back edges of the wings up a little.
- If your plane flies too far to the right, bend the rudder a little to the left.
- If your plane flies too far to the left, bend the rudder a little to the right.

42

Lincoln School Lunch Calendar

for the week of May 21–25

Monday	Tuesday	Wednesday	Thursday	Friday
May 21	**May 22**	**May 23**	**May 24**	**May 25**
• Deli ham and cheese sandwich with lettuce and tomato* or Vegetarian sandwich**	• Homemade turkey with mashed potatoes and gravy or Veggie burger with lettuce and tomato**	• Fish nuggets with dip or Veggie sticks with hummus**	• Homemade lasagna with meat sauce and vegetable or Vegetarian lasagna**	• Pepperoni pizza* or Cheese pizza**
• Snack mix	• Mixed green salad with veggie sticks on top	• Dinner roll	• Breadstick	• Veggie sticks with dip
• Fruit cup	• Fresh fruit	• Low-fat ice cream or Strawberries with yogurt dip	• Fresh fruit	• Fruit cup

*contains pork **vegetarian selection

"You Can Make Tea With Milk"
from *Morning Meals Around the World*
by Maryellen Gregoire

You Can Make Tea with Milk   Makes 1 serving

What you need: water, a tea bag, milk

What to do:

1. Boil the water. You can boil it in a pan on a stove, or you can place the water in a mug and boil it in a microwave.

2. Place the tea bag in the mug of hot water. Let the tea bag steep in the water for 1 to 2 minutes, then remove the tea bag.

3. Pour a little milk in your tea to make it creamy.

4. When your tea has cooled, you can try this Russian morning treat.

Make sure you have an adult to help you.

"You Can Make Breakfast Quesadillas"
from *Morning Meals Around the World*

by Maryellen Gregoire

You Can Make Mexican Breakfast Quesadillas

Makes 2 servings

What you need:

2 flour tortillas
1 onion
1 jalapeño pepper (optional)
1/2 cup (120 grams) shredded
    cheddar cheese
2 thin slices of ham
1 cup (240 grams) sour cream
1 cup (240 grams) salsa

What to do:

1. Place 1 tortilla on
   a microwave-safe plate.

2. Cut the onion into small pieces.

3. Cut the jalapeño pepper
   (if using) into small pieces.

4. Place the shredded cheese, the
   slices of ham, and the pieces of
   onion (and jalapeño pepper, if
   using), on the tortilla.

5. Cover with another tortilla.

6. Microwave on medium heat until the cheese
   has melted.

7. If you like, use any leftover ingredients to decorate your quesadilla.

8. Cut the quesadilla into wedges and serve with sour cream and salsa.

Make sure you have an adult to help you.

Recipe with Text Features

Name:

> **Write a recipe for a simple food or drink. Include at least two text features in your recipe.**

> **List the text features you included in your recipe.**

_____

_____

_____

_____

from *Flashy Fantastic Rain Forest Frogs*

by Dorothy Hinshaw Patent

Frogs need homes to live in. When forests are cut down, frogs and other animals have no place to live, so they die out. Frogs that live in a limited area are especially threatened. The blue poison frog, for example, is found only in small parts of forest in the South American country of Suriname. If its home is destroyed by people harvesting wood, this frog will become extinct.

Frogs have been on Earth for more than 150 million years. But today, frogs are disappearing quickly from some parts of the planet. No one is sure why. Some fear that the increase in ultraviolet light reaching Earth may be to blame. Whatever is killing frogs could be a danger for other forms of life, too. Scientists are working hard to understand what is happening, so that the beauty and usefulness of frogs will always be with us.

What I Wonder

About *Flashy Fantastic Rain Forest Frogs*

> **Write what you wonder about *Flashy Fantastic Rain Forest Frogs*. Write your ideas as questions or as "I wonder" statements.**

_____

_____

_____

_____

_____

_____

_____

_____

_____

_____

_____

_____

What I Wonder

About My Text

Title of Text _____

> **Write at least two things you wonder about the topic of your independent reading text before you read today. Write your ideas as questions or as "I wonder" statements.**

_____

_____

_____

_____

_____

_____

_____

_____

_____

_____

What I Wonder

Stop and Ask Questions
About Deserts (1)

Name:

At each stop, write your questions in the box.

STOP 1

STOP 2

Stop and Ask Questions
About Deserts (2)

At each stop, write your questions in the box.

STOP 1

STOP 2

STOP 3

     Making Meaning®   **51**

Stop and Ask Questions

About Deserts (3)

At each stop, write your questions in the box.

STOP 1

STOP 2

STOP 3

Double-entry Journal

About "Polar Bears in Peril"

Name:

What I Learned

What I Wonder

POLAR BEARS IN PERIL

Arctic sea ice is melting, making it harder for polar bears to survive in the wild.

By Elizabeth Winchester

Polar bears' features help them survive in the Arctic. A thick layer of fat helps keep the bears warm.

The top of the world is a wintry wonderland. Icebergs float in the cold Arctic Ocean. In the deep of winter, the temperature often falls to –30 degrees Fahrenheit and the sun never rises. The ocean is surrounded by frozen ground. There are few people or trees, but to polar bears, the Arctic is home.

Polar bears have thick fur, huge paws, and other features that make them well prepared for life in their harsh environment. In fact, they need the Arctic sea ice for survival. But climate change is causing larger and larger areas of summer sea ice to melt. Experts say that if warming patterns continue, the Arctic could be free of summer sea ice by 2050. That may cause two-thirds of the world's 20,000 polar bears to be gone by then, too.

"Global climate change may not be affecting you, but it is really affecting polar bears in the Arctic," Jeffrey Bonner, president of the St. Louis Zoo in Missouri, told TFK (*TIME for Kids*). Bonner is working with zoo and aquarium officials across the country to prevent the bears from dying out.

The Importance of the Ice

Polar bears can't survive for long on land. Seals are their main source of food. The bears hunt for seals in openings in the sea ice. Polar bears need the ice to get to their prey. In summer, the polar bears that live on land eat very little and wait for the sea ice to return.

54

With the sea ice forming later in the year and melting earlier, polar bears do not have enough opportunity to hunt and eat. Less sea ice makes it harder for the bears to catch the seals. The bears must swim longer distances between ice packs, and they can't always make it. The ice is also getting thinner. These conditions can cause polar bear cubs to become separated from their mothers, who provide them with food.

What Zoos—and You— Can Do

Less ice and snow in the far north is also making the entire planet warmer. Steven Amstrup is the chief scientist of Polar Bears International, a group that is dedicated to saving the bears and their habitat. "The more people who see polar bears and understand their plight, the better the chance we'll alter our warming path in time to save them," he says.

Few people have the chance to see polar bears in the wild. That's where zoos come in. The St. Louis Zoo in Missouri and the North Carolina Zoo in Asheboro both recently opened new polar bear exhibits. "If you save the polar bears, you are doing something dramatic to help the environment," says Bonner.

While there are obstacles to bringing polar bears into the country, Bonner and others are working to show how rescuing orphaned cubs could help the species survive. Zoos would provide the cubs with a safe home. Experts would work to breed the bears and keep polar-bear populations healthy.

You can do your part, too, by protecting the environment and helping efforts to save the bears' habitat. Turn off lights and appliances, and save energy in other ways. "If everybody does small things, that adds up," says Bonner.

Banning TAG

Imagine that you are being chased. You run as fast as you can, but you are not quick enough. You feel hands on your back, touching you. You trip, fall down, skinning your knee. Not again! You are tired of always being "it."

Has this ever happened to you? If it has, you know that it does not feel very good. Some principals, teachers, and parents are worried that playing tag at recess is too dangerous. They argue that kids run into one another, fall down, and get hurt playing tag. They say that sometimes tag leads to hitting, pushing, and bullying. In response to these concerns, schools all over the country are banning the game of tag during recess.

The Other Side

Some parents and kids think schools should not ban tag. A third-grader from the state of Washington even started a petition to get his principal to change the ban and let the kids play tag again at recess. There are a lot of good things about the game. It is easy to get started because you do not need anything to play except some friends. Also, while you run around, you are getting exercise and having fun at the same time. Many people are upset that recess has to be ruined for everyone just because a few children play too rough. After all, the game of tag has been around for hundreds of years.

Different Types of Tag

There are many different versions of tag. You probably know how to play some of them. One of the most popular versions of tag is "freeze tag," where instead of being "it" when you are caught, you have to stand still until another player touches you. There is also "tunnel tag," which is like freeze tag except that your teammate must crawl through your legs before you can play again.

"Monster tag" starts with one person chasing all the others. As each player is tagged, he or she joins hands with "it" to help chase the others. In the end, there is a long chain of players who are all "it," working together. With all the hands and feet, the chain reminds some people of a monster! That is how this kind of tag got its name.

Other Games

If your school does not allow tag at recess, there are lots of other games you can play instead! If you have a ball, you can organize a game of kickball or four square. With a piece of chalk and a few pebbles, you can play hopscotch. You can probably think of many more fun things to do during recess.

Whatever you are allowed to do at recess, it is important that you play fair and are gentle with others. When everyone feels safe, everyone can have fun!

Smile—You've Got Homework!

"Homework." Now there's a word that can put a frown on your face! Many kids don't like doing it. Busy teachers don't always have time to plan it or grade it. Many exhausted parents have to remind their children to do it. If homework causes so much unhappiness, then why do teachers assign it? One simple reason: Homework helps kids learn. A 2006 study showed that children who do homework do better on class tests. That's one benefit of homework. Here are some others.

Practice Makes Perfect

As any kindergarten teacher will tell you, students need to practice saying their ABCs in order to learn them. In fact, practice is necessary to learn most of what is taught in school. Unfortunately, there is not enough time in the school day for students to practice all that they learn. That's what homework is for. Homework provides the practice time that students need.

Homework also helps a teacher teach more effectively. Reviewing homework assignments helps the teacher know what the students understand and what they don't. With this information, teachers can decide whether to reteach a lesson or move on.

Homework helps students practice what they are learning in school.

Memorizing Facts

Like it or not, memorization is an important part of learning in school. Students need to memorize math facts, how words are spelled, historical dates, and other information. But memorizing information—like practicing skills—takes up valuable class time. Having students memorize facts for homework gives teachers more time during the school day for actual teaching. In addition, students don't always need a teacher's help to memorize information. Why waste the teacher's time with this type of schoolwork?

Organization and Planning

Homework can help kids learn how to organize and plan their time. Students with homework must set aside time to get it done. Other activities, like spending time with friends or watching TV, may have to wait until homework is done.

Homework also helps kids learn how to prioritize tasks—or decide which tasks must be done and in what order—and how to plan for how long each task should take. Skills like these are very important to academic success.

School and Home

Homework gives parents a chance to become more involved in their children's school lives. Parents can help with homework while talking with their kids about what they are learning. Parents can also make homework more fun and interesting, and they can help their children see the importance of the work they are doing.

So smile when you hear the word "homework." It's good for you!

Homework provides an opportunity for parents and kids to work together.

Homework— Who Needs It?

Is homework good for kids? Do kids learn more if they do homework? Teachers, students, and parents have been debating these questions for years. Many studies have looked at the impact of homework on student learning, but there is no clear evidence that homework helps students learn more. In fact, one 2012 study found no significant relationship between time spent on homework and grades. That's one argument against homework, but it's not the only one. Let's take a look at some others.

Let Kids Be Kids

Students spend about seven hours a day in school. Most of that time they are thinking, listening, reading, and writing—pretty exhausting stuff! Kids have little time during the school day to relax or spend time with friends. When children get home from school, they need time to unwind. They do not need to do more schoolwork! Most adults don't come home from a full day at work and do even more work for their job. So why should kids?

Kids need time to be kids after school.

Let Families Be Families

Homework is a burden for kids, but it can be a burden for moms and dads, too. After a long day, parents are tired. The last thing they want to do is to keep reminding their reluctant children, "Do your homework!" Homework can be confusing or difficult, and parents don't always have time to help. This means that kids must sometimes struggle through hard homework assignments on their own—and moms and dads are left feeling guilty for not helping. This is stress that busy families don't need.

Families need time to do enjoyable things together. Many children and their parents say goodbye in the morning and often don't see each other again until after five o'clock. That leaves only a few hours for family time before going to bed. It's important for families to spend the little time they have together talking, reading, and doing things they all enjoy.

Who Likes Homework?

If you ask students if they like homework, many will probably say they do not. Because students associate homework with school, negative feelings about homework can turn into negative feelings about school—and disliking school makes learning more difficult.

Is homework worth the stress, family conflict, and loss of interest in learning that it seems to cause? The answer is no.

Homework can cause stress for the whole family.

from *Lifetimes* (1)
by David L. Rice

A lifetime for an army ant is about three years.

Army ants are famous for their ability to work together to accomplish amazing things. They march along like soldiers, sometimes a million at a time. Nothing can stop them. When they come to a river, they make an "ant bridge" of themselves to get across. If the river is very wide, they form large "ant balls" and float to the other side. Army ants eat mostly insects, spiders and small animals, although they have been known to eat horses, cows and even tigers that are tied up or caged. People who live in areas with army ants have to leave their homes for a day or two when the ants come marching through. When they return their houses are completely free of rats, cockroaches, or other pests.

Excerpt from *Lifetimes* by David L. Rice, illustrated by Michael Maydak. Text copyright © 1997 by David L. Rice. Used by permission of Dawn Publications.

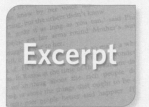

Excerpt

from *Lifetimes* (2)
by David L. Rice

A lifetime for an elephant is about 65 years.

Elephants have feelings much like those you have. They make loud, joyful trumpeting sounds when they meet other elephants. They care for other elephants that are sick or injured. If a baby or friend dies, they show their sadness by refusing to eat or by moaning and crying. Elephants are among the few animals that weep tears when they are very, very sad. Although elephants are the largest animals on land, they don't kill or bother other animals. When ponds and streams dry up, elephants use their trunks to dig down to water. When they finish drinking, they let other animals drink. Without water these animals would die.

Excerpt from *Lifetimes* by David L. Rice, illustrated by Michael Maydak. Text copyright © 1997 by David L. Rice. Used by permission of Dawn Publications.

Name:

> **What do you think is most important to understand and remember from the passage about elephants? Share your thinking with your partner. Then write your ideas on the lines below.**

_____

_____

_____

_____

_____

_____

_____

_____

_____

_____

_____

from *Lifetimes* (3)
by David L. Rice

A lifetime for a saguaro cactus is about 100 years.

If water were money, the saguaro (sa-WAR-o) would be rich. The saguaro grows in the desert where it doesn't rain for eight or nine months at a time. The temperature can get as hot as 120° F. Most plants can't live in such a hot, dry place. But when it does rain, the saguaro saves as much as it can. It stores up to 250 gallons of water in its thick stem to keep it alive until the next rain. Where most plants can't grow at all, the saguaro thrives and grows up to 60 feet tall. The saguaro shares its wealth. Many desert animals depend on the saguaro for food and moisture. Native Americans who live in the desert use its juicy red fruit to make jam or syrup.

Excerpt from *Lifetimes* by David L. Rice, illustrated by Michael Maydak. Text copyright © 1997 by David L. Rice. Used by permission of Dawn Publications.

Think, Pair, Write
About Saguaro Cactuses

What do you think is most important to understand and remember from the passage about saguaro cactuses? Share your thinking with your partner. Then write your ideas on the lines below.

_____

_____

_____

_____

_____

_____

_____

_____

_____

_____

_____

_____

_____

from *Lifetimes* (4)
by David L. Rice

A lifetime for a hermit crab is about five years.

Hermit crabs are very good at taking action to make their lives better. Nature doesn't give them a shell for protection, so they find shells that are empty and recycle them. They use these shells like "motor homes" until the crabs get too big for them. Then they move into larger shells. Another neat trick of the hermit crab is to put a sea anemone on top of its shell. The poisonous arms of the anemone keep the octopus or squid from eating the crab for dinner. Since sea anemones can't move around very well by themselves, "piggy-backing" on the crab is a special treat that allows them to find food as the crab moves along.

Excerpt from *Lifetimes* by David L. Rice, illustrated by Michael Maydak. Text copyright © 1997 by David L. Rice. Used by permission of Dawn Publications.

Name:

> **What do you think is most important to understand and remember from the passage about hermit crabs? Write your ideas on the lines below.**

_____

_____

_____

_____

_____

_____

_____

_____

_____

_____

_____

_____

_____

The Young Rooster
by Arnold Lobel

A young Rooster was summoned to his Father's bedside.

"Son, my time has come to an end," said the aged bird. "Now it is your turn to crow up the morning sun each day."

The young Rooster watched sadly as his Father's life slipped away.

Early the next morning, the young Rooster flew up to the roof of the barn. He stood there, facing the east.

"I have never done this before," said the Rooster. "I must try my best." He lifted his head and crowed. A weak and scratchy croak was the only sound he was able to make.

The sun did not come up. Clouds covered the sky, and a damp drizzle fell all day. All of the animals of the farm came to the Rooster.

"This is a disaster!" cried a Pig.

"We need our sunshine!" shouted a Sheep.

"Rooster, you must crow much louder," said a Bull. "The sun is ninety-three million miles away. How do you expect it to hear you?"

Very early the next morning, the young Rooster flew up to the roof of the barn again. He took a deep breath, he threw back his head and CROWED. It was the loudest crow that was ever crowed since the beginning of roosters.

The animals on the farm were awakened from their sleep with a start.

"What a noise!" cried the Pig.

"My ears hurt!" shouted the Sheep.

"My head is splitting!" said the Bull.

"I am sorry," said the Rooster, "but I was only doing my job."

He said this with a great deal of pride, for he saw, far to the east, the tip of the morning sun coming up over the trees.

Think, Pair, Write
About "The Young Rooster"

Name:

> **What is a theme, or lesson, in this fable? Share your thinking with your partner and then write it on the lines below. Remember to give reasons from the story to support your thinking.**

_____

_____

_____

_____

_____

_____

_____

_____

_____

_____

_____

_____

_____

The Mouse at the Seashore
by Arnold Lobel

A Mouse told his mother and father that he was going on a trip to the seashore.

"We are very alarmed!" they cried. "The world is full of terrors. You must not go!"

"I have made my decision," said the Mouse firmly. "I have never seen the ocean, and it is high time that I did. Nothing can make me change my mind."

"Then we cannot stop you," said Mother and Father Mouse, "but do be careful!"

The next day, in the first light of dawn, the Mouse began his journey. Even before the morning had ended, the Mouse came to know trouble and fear.

A Cat jumped out from behind a tree.

"I will eat you for lunch," he said.

It was a narrow escape for the Mouse. He ran for his life, but he left a part of his tail in the mouth of the Cat.

By afternoon the Mouse had been attacked by birds and dogs. He had lost his way several times. He was bruised and bloodied. He was tired and frightened.

At evening the Mouse slowly climbed the last hill and saw the seashore spreading out before him. He watched the waves rolling onto the beach, one after another. All the colors of the sunset filled the sky.

"How beautiful!" cried the Mouse. "I wish that Mother and Father were here to see this with me."

The moon and the stars began to appear over the ocean. The Mouse sat silently on the top of the hill. He was overwhelmed by a feeling of deep peace and contentment.

The Camel Dances
by Arnold Lobel

The Camel had her heart set on becoming a ballet dancer.

"To make every movement a thing of grace and beauty," said the Camel. "That is my one and only desire."

Again and again she practiced her pirouettes, her relevés, and her arabesques. She repeated the five basic positions a hundred times each day. She worked for long months under the hot desert sun. Her feet were blistered, and her body ached with fatigue, but not once did she think of stopping.

At last the Camel said, "Now I am a dancer." She announced a recital and danced before an invited group of camel friends and critics. When her dance was over, she made a deep bow.

There was no applause.

"I must tell you frankly," said a member of the audience, "as a critic and a spokesman for this group, that you are lumpy and humpy. You are baggy and bumpy. You are, like the rest of us, simply a camel. You are *not* and never will be a ballet dancer!"

Chuckling and laughing, the audience moved away across the sand.

"How very wrong they are!" said the Camel. "I have worked hard. There can be no doubt that I am a splendid dancer. I will dance and dance just for myself."

That is what she did. It gave her many years of pleasure.

Excerpt from *Fables* by Arnold Lobel. Copyright © 1980 by Arnold Lobel. Used by permission of HarperCollins Publishers.

Possum's Tail

from *Pushing Up the Sky* by Joseph Bruchac

Possum's Tail

Cherokee

The Cherokee people originally lived in the area now known as the states of Georgia, Tennessee, and North Carolina. Because they adapted so quickly to the European way of life, they became known as one of the "civilized tribes." However, long before the coming of Europeans they had a sophisticated form of government and lived in large, well-organized villages.

In the early 1800's many Cherokee people were forced to leave their homes and move to Indian Territory by traveling the infamous Trail of Tears. Today Cherokee people live all over the United States, but their two contemporary tribal governments are in Oklahoma and North Carolina. Wily, wise Rabbit is still their favorite trickster character.

(continues)

Possum's Tail (continued)

Characters

NARRATOR

BEAR

RABBIT

TURTLE

RACCOON

POSSUM

OTTER

CRICKET

Note: If more children wish to take part in the play, other animals, such as Deer, Owl, Chipmunk, Squirrel, Beaver, or Fox, can be represented as non-speaking parts.

Props/Scenery

The forest can be suggested by a painted backdrop or potted plants.

A bandage is needed for Possum's tail.

A medicine bottle or **bowl** is also needed for Possum's tail.

The oak tree for Scene III can be painted on a backdrop.

Costumes

Narrator wears a turban made of patterned cloth.

Animal roles can be represented by masks made from paper plates decorated with markers, yarn, cotton balls, beads, etc. The mask can be held by hand in front of the wearer's face or mounted on a handle like a fan.

Possum's furry tail can be made of dark socks stuffed with cotton and stitched together.

Possum's rattail for Scene III can be a long piece of rope.

(continues)

Scene I: The Forest

A group of animals stands together.

NARRATOR: Long ago Possum had the most beautiful tail of all the animals. Everyone knew that was true. And if anyone didn't know, then Possum would tell him so.

BEAR: Tomorrow we will have a big meeting. Rabbit, you be the messenger. Go tell all the animals. We will meet at the big oak tree when Grandmother Sun rises up into the sky.

RABBIT: What will the meeting be about?

BEAR: We will decide that tomorrow.

TURTLE: Oh no, here comes Possum!

RACCOON: He is going to brag about his tail again. I can tell.

Possum enters and walks over to the other animals, holding his long tail in front of him.

POSSUM: *Siyo!* (see-yo) Hello! This day is beautiful. And so is my tail. Look at my beautiful tail.

OTHER ANIMALS: *Siyo,* Possum.

POSSUM: Did you say there would be a meeting tomorrow?

BEAR: Yes.

POSSUM: Then I should speak at the meeting.

TURTLE: Why?

OTTER: Turtle, don't ask him! He'll just talk about his—

POSSUM: Because of my beautiful tail. It is the most beautiful of all. It is not short like Bear's tail. It is long and silky. It is not stiff like Raccoon's tail. It is soft and lovely. It is not stubby like Rabbit's tail. It

(continues)

is fluffy and big. It is not ugly like Turtle's tail. It is pretty and nice. *(Possum can continue to improvise while Bear and Rabbit speak, saying "Isn't it beautiful?" etc.)*

As Possum goes on talking, the other animals yawn and roll their eyes. One by one they fall to the ground and pretend to sleep. During this activity Rabbit taps Bear on the shoulder, and Rabbit and Bear step toward the audience. Possum does not notice, but keeps talking.

RABBIT: I have an idea about Possum.

BEAR: We should stuff moss into our ears so we cannot hear him?

RABBIT: No, I have a better idea than that. Let me whisper it to you.

(continues)

Rabbit whispers into Bear's ear. Bear smiles and nods.

BEAR: That is a good idea.

Bear and Rabbit turn back toward Possum, who is still talking. The other animals are still pretending to sleep, but Possum doesn't notice.

RABBIT: Possum, you *do* have a beautiful tail.

POSSUM: Yes. That is true. Shall I tell you about it?

BEAR: No! I mean, not now.

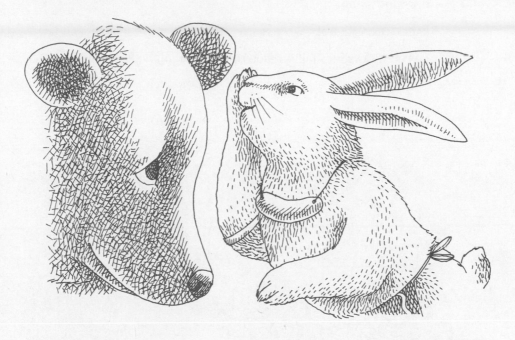

RABBIT: We have decided that you should be the first speaker at the big meeting tomorrow.

POSSUM: Of course. That is true. The one with the most beautiful tail

(continues)

should always speak first.

RABBIT: Possum, your tail should look its best for the meeting.

POSSUM: Of course. That is true. My tail should look its best.

RABBIT: I will take you to Cricket. He will put some special medicine on your tail. Then your tail will be ready for the meeting.

POSSUM: Of course. That is true. Let us go to Cricket.

Possum and Rabbit go offstage together. The other animals open their eyes and sit up.

RACCOON: Oh, no!

OTTER: If Possum's tail is made more beautiful, he'll never stop talking.

(continues)

Possum's Tail (continued)

TURTLE: Otter is right. We'll all have to move away to escape his bragging.

BEAR: Don't worry. Rabbit has a plan.

Scene II: Another Part of the Forest

Cricket crouches on the ground.

RABBIT: Cricket, I want you to put some of your *special* medicine on Possum's tail.

POSSUM: Yes. That is true. I want my tail to look even more beautiful.

CRICKET: Rabbit, do you mean my *special* medicine?

RABBIT: Yes, I mean your *special* medicine.

POSSUM: Hurry up. I want you to fix my tail.

CRICKET: I will fix it. *(Cricket pretends to apply medicine to Possum's tail from either a bottle or a bowl.)* This medicine will make your tail look as it has never looked before.

POSSUM: Will everyone notice it?

CRICKET: Oh yes, everyone will notice it. *(Cricket wraps a bandage around Possum's tail.)* Now you must keep this old snakeskin wrapped around your tail all night. Do not take it off until you are at the meeting.

(continues)

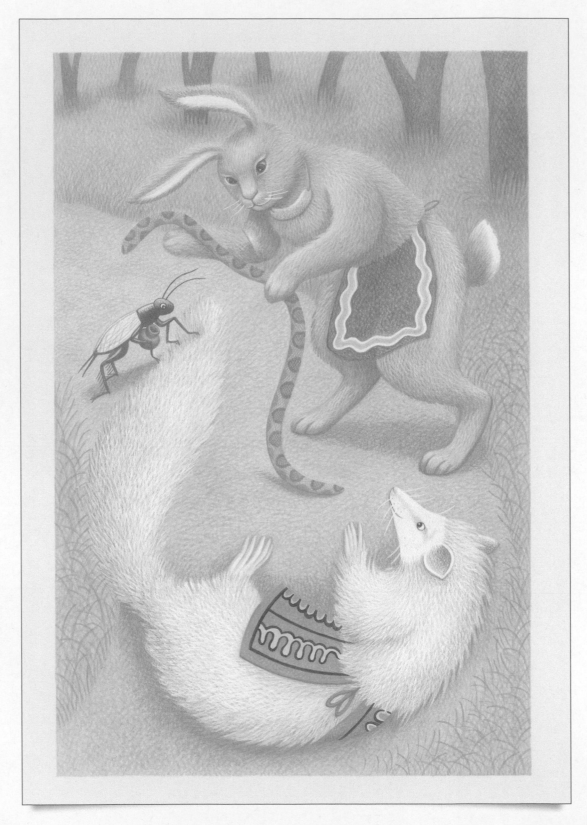

(continues)

Scene III: The Forest, Near the Big Oak Tree

All the animals are gathered in a semicircle. Possum's tail is still wrapped in the snakeskin.

BEAR: Possum will open our meeting.

RABBIT: Everyone, pay attention.

POSSUM: *Siyo,* everyone. I have been asked to speak today because of my tail. It is the most beautiful of all. Here, let me show you how beautiful it is.

Possum unwraps his tail. It now looks like a big rat's tail, but Possum does not notice.

RACCOON: Look at Possum's tail!

POSSUM *(still showing off the tail without looking at it)***:** Yes. Look at my tail. Look at how beautiful it is.

TURTLE: It has no hair at all!

(continues)

OTTER: It is really ugly.

RACCOON: It is funny looking.

The animals begin to laugh. Possum looks at his tail and sees that it has no hair.

POSSUM: My tail! Cricket has ruined it!

Possum sits down on the ground, closes his eyes, and then rolls onto his back with his feet up in the air. He stays there until all the other animals have gone. Then he gets up and runs away.

NARRATOR: So it is that Possum now has the ugliest tail of all the animals. Ever since that time, whenever Possum meets another animal, he closes his eyes, rolls over on his back, and pretends to be dead until the other animal goes away. And Possum no longer brags about his tail!

Think and Write

About a Theme in *Keepers*

Name:

> **What do you think is a theme, or message or lesson, in this story? What in the story makes you think that? Write your ideas on the lines below.**

_____

_____

_____

_____

_____

_____

_____

_____

_____

_____

_____

_____

Thoughts About My Reading Life

Name:

What are some of your favorite kinds of books now? Why?

_____

_____

_____

Where is your favorite place to read?

_____

_____

_____

What does the word *reading* mean to you?

_____

_____

_____

When you don't understand something you are reading, what do you do?

_____

_____

_____

What kinds of books did you read for the first time this year? What topics did you read about for the first time?

_____

_____

Book Recommendation

Name: _____

Book title: _____

Author: _____

What the book is about: _____

_____

_____

_____

_____

_____

Why I like this book: _____

_____

_____

_____

_____

_____

An exciting or interesting part to read aloud (include page numbers):

_____

_____

Summary Reading List

Name:

Book Title	Author	Reminder

List the books you would like to read this summer. For each book, write the title, the author's name, and a few words to remind you what the book is about.

Reading Log

Reading Log

Date	Title	Author
9/25/20	MISS NeLSon HaS a helidaY	JUPan GreenawaY

Comment

Reading Log

Date	Title	Author

Comment

Reading Log

Date	Title	Author

Name:

Comment

Reading Log

Date	Title	Author

Name:

Reading Log

Date	Title	Author

Comment

Reading Log

Date	Title	Author

Comment

Reading Log

Date	Title	Author

Comment

Reading Log

Date	Title	Author

Comment

Reading Log

Date	Title	Author

Comment

Reading Log

Date	Title	Author

Comment

Reading Log

Date	Title	Author

Comment

Reading Log

Date	Title	Author

Name:

Comment

Reading Log

Date	Title	Author

Name:

Comment

Reading Log

Date	Title	Author

Comment

Reading Journal

Reading Journal

Name: _____ Date: _____

_____

_____

_____

_____

_____

_____

_____

_____

_____

_____

_____

_____

_____

_____

Reading Journal

Name: _____   Date: _____

_____

_____

_____

_____

_____

_____

_____

_____

_____

_____

_____

_____

_____

_____

Reading Journal

Name: _____ Date: _____

_____

_____

_____

_____

_____

_____

_____

_____

_____

_____

_____

_____

_____

_____

Reading Journal

Name: _____ Date: _____

_____

_____

_____

_____

_____

_____

_____

_____

_____

_____

_____

_____

_____

_____

_____

Reading Journal

Name: _____ Date: _____

_____

_____

_____

_____

_____

_____

_____

_____

_____

_____

_____

_____

_____

Reading Journal

Name: _____ Date: _____

_____

_____

_____

_____

_____

_____

_____

_____

_____

_____

_____

_____

_____

_____

Reading Journal

Name: _____ Date: _____

_____

_____

_____

_____

_____

_____

_____

_____

_____

_____

_____

_____

_____

Reading Journal

Name: _____ Date: _____

_____

_____

_____

_____

_____

_____

_____

_____

_____

_____

_____

_____

_____

_____

Reading Journal

Name: _____ Date: _____

_____

_____

_____

_____

_____

_____

_____

_____

_____

_____

_____

_____

_____

_____

_____

_____

Reading Journal

Name: _____ Date: _____

_____

_____

_____

_____

_____

_____

_____

_____

_____

_____

_____

_____

_____

_____

_____

_____

Reading Journal

Name: _____ Date: _____

_____

_____

_____

_____

_____

_____

_____

_____

_____

_____

_____

_____

_____

Reading Journal

Name: _____ Date: _____

_____

_____

_____

_____

_____

_____

_____

_____

_____

_____

_____

_____

_____

_____

_____

Reading Journal

Name: _____ Date: _____

_____

_____

_____

_____

_____

_____

_____

_____

_____

_____

_____

_____

_____

_____

_____

Reading Journal

Name: _____ Date: _____

_____

_____

_____

_____

_____

_____

_____

_____

_____

_____

_____

_____

_____

_____

_____

Reading Journal

Name: _____ Date: _____

_____

_____

_____

_____

_____

_____

_____

_____

_____

_____

_____

_____

_____

_____

Reading Journal

Name: _____ Date: _____

_____

_____

_____

_____

_____

_____

_____

_____

_____

_____

_____

_____

_____

_____

_____

Reading Journal

Name: _____ Date: _____

_____

_____

_____

_____

_____

_____

_____

_____

_____

_____

_____

_____

_____

_____

_____

Reading Journal

Name: _____   Date: _____

_____

_____

_____

_____

_____

_____

_____

_____

_____

_____

_____

_____

_____

_____

_____

_____

Reading Journal

Name: _____   Date: _____

_____

_____

_____

_____

_____

_____

_____

_____

_____

_____

_____

_____

_____

Reading Journal

Name: _____   Date: _____

_____

_____

_____

_____

_____

_____

_____

_____

_____

_____

_____

_____

_____

Reading Journal

Name: _____   Date: _____

_____

_____

_____

_____

_____

_____

_____

_____

_____

_____

_____

_____

_____

_____

_____

Reading Journal

Name: _____ Date: _____

_____

_____

_____

_____

_____

_____

_____

_____

_____

_____

_____

_____

_____

_____

Reading Journal

Name: _____ Date: _____

_____

_____

_____

_____

_____

_____

_____

_____

_____

_____

_____

_____

_____

Reading Journal

Name: _____ Date: _____

_____

_____

_____

_____

_____

_____

_____

_____

_____

_____

_____

_____

_____

Reading Journal

Name: _____ Date: _____

_____

_____

_____

_____

_____

_____

_____

_____

_____

_____

_____

_____

_____

_____

_____